THOUGHTS
of
CHAIRMAN
BUFFETT

THIRTY YEARS OF
UNCONVENTIONAL
WISDOM FROM THE
SAGE OF OMAHA

THOUGHTS

of

CHAIRMAN

BUFFETT

◆

THIRTY YEARS OF UNCONVENTIONAL WISDOM FROM THE SAGE OF OMAHA

◆

COMPILED BY SIIMON REYNOLDS

HarperBusiness
A Division of HarperCollinsPublishers

THOUGHTS OF CHAIRMAN BUFFETT. Copyright © 1998 by Siimon Reynolds. All rights reserved. Printed in the United States of America. No part of this book may be used or reproduced in any manner whatsoever without written permission except in the case of brief quotations embodied in critical articles and reviews. For information address HarperCollins Publishers, Inc., 10 East 53rd Street, New York, NY 10022.

HarperCollins books may be purchased for educational, business, or sales promotional use. For information please write: Special Markets Department, HarperCollins Publishers, Inc., 10 East 53rd Street, New York, NY 10022.

FIRST EDITION

Designed by Elina D. Nudelman

Library of Congress Cataloging–in–Publication Data

Buffett, Warren.
    Thoughts of chairman buffett : thirty years of unconventional wisdom from the sage of Omaha / compiled by Siimon Reynolds.
        p. cm
    ISBN 0-88730-890-2
    1. Buffett, Warren — Quotations. 2. Capitalists and financiers — United States. 3. Biography.
I. Reynolds, Siimon. II. Title
HG172.B84 B839 1998
332.621   97-41278

97 98 99 00 01 ❖/RRD 10 9 8 7 6 5 4 3 2 1

CONTENTS

Introduction

He has been called the Wizard of Omaha, the Sage of the West, the King of Kiewit Plaza. He is Warren Buffett, the greatest investor who ever lived.

Ensconced in his humble office, without even putting his name on the building and with just a handful of aides, Warren Buffett has become the second richest man in America.

Indeed, had you the perspicacity to invest $10,000 with young Warren in 1956, your little nest egg would now be a tyrannosaurus egg worth over $80,000,000! That's an average yearly return of 26.7 percent on your money every year for thirty years. To say success like this is rarely heard of is a massive understatement. It is so rare that some experts call Buffett a "Five Sigma Event," meaning he's so unusual he should be left out of the statistics as a freak of nature, never to happen again.

But Buffett is still happening. In fact, his last ten years' return on money invested is a whopping 32.36 percent! Sure beats putting it in the bank.

So how on earth does Buffett do it?

Well, it may not be easy, but it *is* simple. Buffett follows some basic rules, which I shall elucidate at the end of this book— rules anyone can follow to become an above-average investor. He also has a unique homespun philosophy about the making of money.

Inside this little book is thirty years of vintage Buffett: the lessons he's learned;

the mistakes he's made; his observations about people, life, business, and, of course, making a buck. If you ever wanted to learn from a money master but couldn't stomach those long-winded finance books, *Thoughts of Chairman Buffett* is for you. It's short, powerful, and to the point.

When you read his words, take a while to consider their deeper meaning. On almost every page is a thought with the potential to lift your investment game or bring a wayward business back on track.

Another thing about Buffett: He's easy to understand. This is not one of those investors who sweat over reams of statistical charts and fiscal hieroglyphics. This is a guy who doesn't even use a computer. He relies on information you and I can get our hands on—annual reports, newspaper and magazine articles, and commonly available financial records. What makes him an investment genius is how he looks at this information. You'll get a real sense of that from the sage advice in this book.

So here it is—straight from the silver-haired, crumpled-suited magician's mouth—the secrets to investment success.

ON HOW TO GET WEALTHY

"I will tell you the secret of getting rich on Wall Street. You try to be greedy when others are fearful, and you try to be very fearful when others are greedy."

—Roger Lowenstein, *Buffett: The Making of an American Capitalist*

ON HIRING

"Somebody once said that in looking for people to hire, you look for three qualities: integrity, intelligence, and energy. And if they don't have the first, the other two will kill you."

—*Omaha World Herald*, February 1, 1994

ON INDEPENDENCE

"You have to think for yourself. It always amazes me how high-IQ people mindlessly imitate. I never get good ideas talking to other people."

—*U.S. News & World Report*, June 20, 1994

ON THE FUTURE OF INTEREST RATES

"Only two people understand that. Both of them live in Switzerland. However, they're diametrically opposed to each other."

—Roger Lowenstein, *Buffett: The Making of an American Capitalist*

ON INTELLIGENCE

"You don't need to be a rocket scientist.
Investing is not a game where the guy
with the 160 IQ beats the guy with
the 130 IQ."

—*Fortune,* 1989

ON LOVING YOUR WORK

"You know, some days I get up and
I want to *tap*-dance."

—Attribution by bridge partner
Judge John Grant

ON PERCEPTION VERSUS REALITY

"Maybe grapes from a little eight-acre vineyard in France are really the best in the whole world, but I have always had a suspicion that about 99 percent of it is in the telling and about 1 percent is in the drinking."

—Roger Lowenstein, *Buffett: The Making of an American Capitalist*

ON HAVING MENTORS

"The best thing I did was to choose
the right heroes."

—Roger Lowenstein, *Buffett: The Making of an
American Capitalist*

ON EGO

"My ego is wrapped up with Berkshire.
No question about that."

—*Fortune*, April 11, 1988

On People

"I shave my face on the same side every morning and put on the same shoe first and people are creatures of habit."

—*Courier Express v. Evening News,*
testimony, of Warren Buffett, pp. 44–45,
November 4, 1977

On the Advantage of Chaos

"The future is never clear; you pay a very high price in the stock market for a cheery consensus. Uncertainty actually is the friend of the buyer of long-term values."

—*Forbes*, August 6, 1979

ON REAL ESTATE

"Why should I buy real estate when the
stock market is so easy?"

—Roger Lowenstein, *Buffett: The Making of an
American Capitalist*

ON JUNK BONDS

"I personally think, before it's all over,
junk bonds will live up to their name."

—*Omaha World-Herald*, May 22, 1984

ON SUPPORTING KIDS

"My kids are going to carve out their own place in this world, and they know I'm there for them whatever they want to do."

—*Fortune,* September 29, 1986

ON BORROWING

"It's a very sad thing. You can have some-body whose aggregate performance is ter-rific, but if they have a weakness—maybe it's with alcohol, maybe it's susceptibility to taking a little easy money—it's the weak link that snaps you. And frequently, in the financial markets, the weak link is borrowed money."

—Roger Lowenstein, *Buffett: The Making of an American Capitalist*

ON VISUALIZING SUCCESS
AT AGE SEVEN

"I don't have much money now but
someday I will and I'll have my picture
in the paper."

—Attribution by Leila Buffett

On Asking the Right Questions
A Story About a Stranger Patting a Dog

"The fellow wanted to get acquainted with folks, so he went over to the village square and saw an old-timer with a kind of a mean-looking German shepherd.

He looked at the dog a little tentatively and he said, "Does your dog bite?" The old-timer said, "Nope." So the stranger reached down to pet him and the dog lunged at him and practically took off his arm, and the stranger as he was repairing his shredded coat turned to the old-timer and said, "I thought you said your dog doesn't bite." The guy says, "Ain't my dog."

—Roger Lowenstein, *Buffett: The Making of an American Capitalist*

ON TIME MANAGEMENT

"That which is not worth doing is not worth doing well."

—John Train, *The Midas Touch*

ON MARKET PREDICTIONS

"I have never met a man who could forecast the market."

— Roger Lowenstein, *Buffett: The Making of an American Capitalist*

On the Two Biggest Rules
of Investing

"Rule No. 1: Never lose money."
"Rule No. 2: Never forget Rule No. 1."

—*Forbes 400*, October 27, 1986

ON CHOOSING INVESTMENTS

"It's like when you marry a girl. Is it her eyes? Her personality? It's a whole bunch of things you can't separate."

— *The Wall Street Journal,* March 16, 1989

ON WHY COKE IS A GREAT INVESTMENT
(1)

"If you gave me a hundred billion dollars and said, Take away the soft-drink leadership of Coca-Cola in the world, I'd give it back to you and say it can't be done."

—*Fortune*, May 31, 1993

ON GROWING UP

"Someday you're going to have to tell
your dad to go to hell."

—Roger Lowenstein, *Buffett: The Making of an
American Capitalist*

ON GIVING YOUR KIDS A BIG INHERITANCE

"The idea that you get a lifetime supply of food stamps based on coming out of the right womb strikes at my idea of fairness."

—*Channels* magazine, November 1986

ON WHY COKE IS A GREAT INVESTMENT (2)

"Coke is exactly the kind of company I like. I like products I can understand. I don't know what a transistor is, but I appreciate the contents of a Coke can. Berkshire Hathaway's purchase of stock in the Coca-Cola company was the ultimate case of me putting my money where my mouth was."

—*The Sydney Morning Herald*, October 9, 1993

ON HOW A CORPORATION SHOULD BEHAVE

HAVING JUST BECOME ACTING CHAIRMAN OF SALOMON BROTHERS

"Anything not only on the line, but near the line, will be called out."

—*The Wall Street Journal*, August 19, 1991

ON MORAL INTEGRITY

"I want employees to ask themselves whether they are willing to have any contemplated act appear on the front page of their local paper the next day, to be read by their spouses, children and friends. . . . If they follow this test, they need not fear my other message to them: Lose money for the firm and I will be understanding; lose a shred of reputation for the firm, and I will be ruthless."

—Statement to House Subcommittee
Investigating Salomon Brothers,
September, 11, 1991

ON CHOOSING STAFF

"In the end we must have people to match
our principles, not the reverse."

—Salomon Brothers report to shareholders,
third quarter 1991

ON PLAYING IT STRAIGHT

"Good profits simply are not inconsistent
with good behavior."

—Salomon Brothers report to shareholders,
third quarter 1991

ON RISK
(1)

"We've done better by avoiding dragons rather than by slaying them."

—Andrew Kilpatrick, *Of Permanent Value*

ON DEBT

"You're looking at a fellow who owes $70,000 on a second home in Laguna, and I've got that because of the low rate ... and that's all I've owed for I don't know how many years. If you're smart, you don't need debt. If you're dumb, it's poisonous."

—Andrew Kilpatrick, *Of Permanent Value*

ON IDEAL COMPANIES

"Good businesses are the ones that in some way are reasonably sheltered from competition. That gets to having what I call a franchise of some sort."

—*Financial Review,* December 9, 1985

ON BERKSHIRE'S ACQUISITION POLICY

"It's very scientific. We just sit around and wait for the phone to ring. Sometimes it's a wrong number."

—Andrew Kilpatrick, *Of Permanent Value*

ON TRADITIONAL WISDOM

"Traditional wisdom can be long on
tradition and short on wisdom."

—Source unknown

ON WALL STREET

"If you want to make money, hold your
nose and go to Wall Street."

—Financial Review, February 14, 1992

ON POSSESSIONS

"There's nothing material I want
very much."

—*Esquire,* June 1988

ON INVESTING IN COMPUTER STOCKS

"Bill Gates is a good friend, and I think he may be the smartest guy I've ever met. But I don't know what those little things [computers] do."

—*Forbes*, October 18, 1993

ON FAME

"Complete anonymity would be the best way for me to operate, but because of size that's not possible anymore."

—*Financial Review*, December 9, 1985

ON SELF-ESTEEM

"I've never had any self-doubt. I have never been discouraged."

—*U.S. News & World Report,* June 20, 1994

ON HAVING MARGINS FOR ERROR

"This is the cornerstone of our investment philosophy: Never count on making a good sale. Have the purchase price be so attractive that even a mediocre sale gives good results."

—Roger Lowenstein, *Buffett: The Making of an American Capitalist*

ON CONSISTENCY

"Let's go back to that restaurant. Why take the risk with another place? We know exactly what we're going to get."

—*Fortune 1990 Investors Guide*

ON JAIL

"I always say I wouldn't mind going to jail
if I had three cellmates who played
bridge."

—Andrew Kilpatrick, *Of Permanent Value*

On Food

"My ideas about food and diet were irrevocably formed quite early—the product of a wildly successful party that celebrated my fifth birthday. On that occasion we had hot dogs, hamburgers, soft drinks, popcorn, and ice cream. I found complete gastronomical fulfillment in this array and have seen no reason subsequently to expand my horizons."

—*First Gentleman's Cookbook* by
William D. Orr, page 178

ON LEAVING MONEY TO YOUR KIDS

"As Jesse Owen's child, your development would not be facilitated by letting you start 100-yard dashes at the 50-yard line."

— *Warren Buffett Speaks,* Janet Lowe

ON WHEN TO BUY SHARES

"A great investment opportunity occurs when a marvelous business encounters a onetime huge but solvable problem."

—Source unknown

ON THE DANGERS OF PERCEPTIONS

"It's only when the tide goes out that you learn who's been swimming naked."

—Andrew Kilpatrick, *Of Permanent Value*

HOW BUFFETT STARTED

Born in 1930 to a petite midwestern lass named Leila and her arrow-straight husband, Howard, Buffett was no whiz kid at school. After class, however, was a different story. Buffett and his wily teenage accomplices bought pinball machines, did newspaper runs, and even wrote a horse betting tip sheet (*Stable-Boy Selections*). This after-hours entrepreneurship worked, and by age fifteen not only was Warren pulling in around $40 a week, he'd already bought himself forty acres of land. Upon graduating from high school at sixteen, Warren Buffett had saved around $5,000. (Remember, we are talking 1947 dollars.)

University beckoned. Electing to take a degree in finance at the Wharton School of Business at the University of Pennsylvania, Warren spent his spare time learning bridge, reading business books, and playing pranks. But after transferring to the University of Nebraska he happened upon the book that would change his life.

When Warren Buffett read *The Intelligent Investor* by Benjamin Graham he was startled by Ben's insightful mathematical approach and, upon graduating, promptly traveled all the way to the Big Apple to study with Graham (who was then lecturing at Columbia).

Grahamites are a fervent bunch. They believe the crucial first step is to understand a company's basic value; once this is worked out accurately, all one has to do is buy shares in that company at a price significantly below this value. Almost inevitably, they claim, it is only a matter of time before the stock market realizes it has made a boo-boo and pushes the share price up. Sounds simple enough. The trick, of course, is getting the original calculations right, and at that Ben Graham was an ace.

Graham and Buffett were kindred spirits, and it wasn't long before the teacher offered his No. 1 student a full-time job. Warren Buffett was on his way. For the next two years he poured his heart and soul into learning from the investment master, working late into the night and immersing himself in every detail of a target company's performance.

It was an exciting time for Warren, studying with a master and living in the fastest-moving city on earth. But just as things were getting hot for Buffett, the stove was turned off. At age sixty-one. Benjamin Graham decided to cash in his chips and retire.

.This misfortune was in fact a golden opportunity in disguise. Buffett returned to his folks in Omaha, took a big breath, and opened his own investment partnership—at the ripe old age of twenty-five. Thirteen years later, Buffett and his partners had amassed a stunning investment record averaging over 29.5 percent a year.

But just when his peers were frothing with excitement over the market's frenzied growth, the wizard elected to disband the partnership. Where others saw an investment oasis, Buffett saw a desert—one filled with rattlesnakes, at that. His timing, as ever, was perfect. A year later the stock market came to its senses with a mighty thud.

By then Buffett had liquidated all his stocks except two, the bigger holding being Berkshire Hathaway, New England's last manufacturer of textiles. He offered his investors a choice: They could either cash in their stock and make a handsome profit or they could leave it in Berkshire under his control. Some sold at $43 a share and then spent the next three decades kicking themselves. Others stayed in and watched a single share of Berkshire Hathaway soar to over $38,000.

ON CREDIT CARD DEBT

"Nobody's ever gotten rich in this world getting money for 18 to 20 percent."

—Associated Press, November 11, 1997

On Stocks with Good Histories

"The investor of today does not profit
from yesterday's growth."

— *The Commercial and Financial Chronicle,*
December 6, 1951

ON LIQUIDITY

"The worst investments are those where you tie up your money for a long time that you could have been using better someplace else."

—*Financial Review*, December 9, 1985

ON THE SECRET OF SUCCESS

"The key in life is to figure out who to be the batboy for."

—*Broadcasting*, June 9, 1986

ON MANAGEMENT

"Business management can be viewed as a three-act play—the dream, the execution, and the passing of the baton."

—Foreword to *Beating the Odds* by
Leonard H. Goldenson, 1991

ON HIS INVESTMENT IN SEE'S CANDY SHOPS

"When business sags we spread the rumor that our candy acts as an aphrodisiac. Very effective. The rumor, that is; not the candy."

—Andrew Kilpatrick, *Of Permanent Value*

ON RACISM

"Now there are Jewish families that have been in Omaha a hundred years, they have contributed to the community all the time, they have helped build Omaha as much as anybody, and yet they can't join a club that John Jones, the new middle-rank Union Pacific man, joins as soon as he's transferred here. That is hardly fair."

— *Super Money* by Adam Smith, pp 198–199

ON HOW HE BOUGHT A $60-MILLION FURNITURE STORE

"Today is my birthday and I want to buy your store. How much do you want for it?"

—Attribution by *Regardies*, February, 1986

ON BUSINESS SCHOOLS
TALKING ABOUT THE NEBRASKA FURNITURE MART

"Anybody would learn a lot more from watching this business for a few months than from going to business school."

— *The New York Times,* June 17, 1994

On Buying Businesses

"Mentally we're always buying businesses. It's just that sometimes we can buy all of them and sometimes we can only buy little pieces of them."

—*Financial World,* June 13, 1984

ON HINDSIGHT

"There are lots of things I wish I'd done in hindsight. But I don't think much of hindsight generally in terms of investment decisions. You only get paid for what you do."

—*Fortune*

ON COMPANY GOALS

"Many decades ago, J. P. Morgan stated the objective of his firm: 'First-class business run in a first-class way.' I have yet to hear of a better goal."

—Statement to House Committee investigating Salomon Brothers, September 11, 1991

ON WHY HE BOUGHT GILLETTE SHARES

"It's pleasant to go to bed every night knowing there are 2.5 billion males in the world who will have to shave in the morning."

—*Forbes*, October 18, 1993

ON OTHER PEOPLE'S OPINIONS

"One piece of advice I got at Columbia from Ben Graham that I've never forgotten: You're neither right nor wrong because other people agree with you. You're right because your facts are right and your reasoning is right. That's the only thing that makes you right."

—Andrew Kilpatrick, *Of Permanent Value*

ON TAKING YOUR TIME

"I have never been big on leveraging
because I never thought it was important
to make a lot of money next year. I have
always felt that I would make more, but I
have never been in a hurry."

—*Financial Review,* December 9, 1985

ON CHOOSING A BUSINESS

"I want to be in businesses so good that
even a dummy can make money."

—*Fortune,* April 11, 1988

ON THE BEAUTY OF THE INVESTMENT BUSINESS

"Investing is the greatest business in the world because you never have to swing. You stand at the plate; the pitcher throws you General Motors at 47! U.S. Steel at 39! And nobody calls a strike on you. There's no penalty except opportunity. All day you wait for the pitch you like; then, when the fielders are asleep, you step up and hit it."

—*Forbes*, November 1, 1974

ON A TYPICAL DAY

"Well, first of all, I tap-dance into work. And then I sit down and I read. Then I talk on the phone for seven or eight hours. And then I take home more to read. Then I talk on the phone in the evening. We read a lot. We have a general sense of what we're after. We're looking for seven-footers. That's about all there is to it."

—Source unknown

ON THE POWER OF THE PRESS

"Essentially, there is virtually no one, with the exception of an assassin, that can do you as much damage as somebody can in the press if they do something the wrong way."

—*Omaha World-Herald*, September 3, 1992

ON HIS OLD BUSINESS PARTNER, CHARLIE MUNGER

"We plan to be here until we're both sitting here wondering, 'Who's that guy sitting next to me?'"

—Andrew Kilpatrick, *Of Permanent Value*

ON HOW TO VIEW STOCKS

"Look at stocks as businesses, look for
businesses you understand, run by people
you trust and are comfortable with, and
leave them alone for a long time."

—Andrew Kilpatrick, *Of Permanent Value*

ON TIME MANAGEMENT
(2)

"Charlie Munger and I can handle a
four-page memo over the phone with
three grunts."

—John Train, *The Midas Touch*

ON WHY HE DOESN'T GIVE HIS FORTUNE AWAY

"When I'm dead, I assume there'll still be serious problems of a social nature as there are now. Society will get a greater benefit from my money later than if I do it now."

—*Forbes,* October 18, 1993

ON WHEN HE'LL RETIRE

"About five to ten years after I die."

—*Forbes 400,* October 19, 1992

ON CHOOSING A BUSINESS PARTNER

"I think you'll probably start looking for the person that you can always depend on; the person whose ego does not get in his way; the person who's perfectly willing to let someone else take credit for an idea as long as it worked; the person who essentially wouldn't let you down who thought straight as opposed to brilliantly."

—Andrew Kilpatrick, *Of Permanent Value*

ON IDEAS

"All I want is one good idea every year. If you really push me, I will settle for one good idea every two years."

—*Financial Review,* December 9, 1985

ON OPPORTUNITY

"Graham's premise was that there would
periodically be times when you couldn't
find good values, and it's a good idea to
go to the beach."

—*Forbes,* June 13, 1985

ON FEAR

"There is one thing I am scared of. I am afraid to die."

—Roger Lowenstein, *Buffett: The Making of an American Capitalist*

ON NEPOTISM

"Would anyone say the best way to pick a champion Olympic team is to select the sons and daughters of those who won twenty years ago? Giving someone a favored position just because his old man accomplished something is a crazy way for society to compete."

—*Fortune,* September 29, 1986

ON THE IMPORTANCE OF FREEDOM

"I really like my life. I've arranged my life
so that I can do what I want."

—*Regardies*, February 1986

ON ETHICAL INVESTMENT MANAGEMENT

"The investment manager must put his client first in everything he does."

—*Fortune,* 1989

ON THINKING LONG TERM
(1)

"I wouldn't buy any stocks I would not be happy owning if they stopped trading it for three years. If you can find companies that you will want to be an investor for in five or ten years, you'll probably do reasonably well."

—*Money*, 1987

ON MAKING MONEY

"I enjoy the process far more than the proceeds, though I have learned to live with those also."

—*Forbes*, October 22, 1990

ON WALL STREET

"Wall Street is the only place that people ride to in a Rolls-Royce to get advice from those who take the subway."

—*Los Angeles Times Magazine*, April 7, 1991

ON ENJOYING WORK

"I am doing what I would like most to be doing in the world, and I have been since I was 20. I choose to work with every single person I work with. That ends up being the most important factor. I don't interact with people I don't like or admire. That's the key. It's like marrying."

—*Fortune*, September 11, 1989

ON COMPLICATING THINGS

"There seems to be some perverse human characteristic that likes to make easy things difficult."

—Andrew Kilpatrick, *Of Permanent Value*

ON PREDICTING MARKETS

"The fact that people will be full of greed, fear, or folly is predictable. The sequence is not predictable."

—*Channels* magazine, November 1986

ON THE LIMITATIONS OF WEALTH

"Money, to some extent, sometimes lets you be in more interesting environments. But it can't change how many people love you or how healthy you are."

—*Channels* magazine, November 1986

ON LEAVING GOOD
MANAGEMENT ALONE

"At Berkshire we don't tell .400-hitters
how to swing."

—Peter Lynch, *One Up On Wall Street*

ON SIMPLICITY

"Business schools reward complex
behavior more than simple behavior; but
simple behavior is more effective."

—*Channels* magazine, November 1986

ON THINKING LONG TERM
(2)

"We like to buy businesses, but we don't
like to sell them."

—*Omaha World-Herald*, May 21, 1986

ON PEOPLE VERSUS COMPUTERS

"It looks . . . impressive if it comes out of a computer. But it's frequently nonsense. The person who's making the decision is far more important."

—*Outstanding Investor Digest*, October 7, 1987

ON HIS INVESTMENT PHILOSOPHY

"You simply have to behave according to what is rational rather than according to what is fashionable."

—*Fortune*, January 4, 1988

ON PRICE

"It's far better to buy a wonderful company at a fair price than a fair company at a wonderful price."

—Widely quoted

On Bequeathing His Money

"And to Peter, who wants to be mentioned in my will: 'Hi, Pete!'"

—Roger Lowenstein, *Buffett: The Making of an American Capitalist*

ON THE IDEAL INVESTOR PERSONALITY

"The most important quality for an investor is temperament, not intellect. You don't need tons of IQ in this business. You don't have to be able to play three-dimensional chess or duplicate bridge. You need a temperament that derives great pleasure neither from being with the crowd nor against the crowd. You know you're right, not because of the position of others but because your facts and your reasoning are right."

—*Adam Smith's Money World*, June 20, 1988

ON BILL GATES

"Bill Gates could do what I do . . . but I can't do what he does."

—*Los Angeles Times,* February 9, 1998

On Thinking Ahead

"Someone's sitting in the shade today because someone planted a tree a long time ago."

—NewsInc., January 1991

ON CAPITAL

"Easy access to funding tends to cause undisciplined decisions."

—Andrew Kilpatrick, *Of Permanent Value*

ON WHY HE DOESN'T USE A COMPUTER

"I am a computer."

—*The New York Times,* April 1, 1990

ON ADVICE TO STUDENTS

"Go to work for whomever you admire the most. You'll be turned on; you'll feel like getting out of bed in the morning; and you'll learn a lot.... As a corollary, I would never go to work for an operation that I had any negative feelings about."

—Widely quoted

ON CORPORATE RESTRUCTURINGS

"Restructurings—That's a word for mistakes."

—Andrew Kilpatrick, *Of Permanent Value*

ON HIS COMPANY'S FUTURE

"I see a lot of interesting things happening, but I haven't the faintest idea what they'll be."

—*Nightly Business Review,* April 26, 1993

ON INHERITANCE

"Children should be given enough to do what they want to do, but not enough to be idle."

—WOWTTV, Omaha, October 14, 1993

ON HIS STRENGTHS

"I'm rational. Plenty of people have higher IQs and plenty of people work more hours, but I'm rational about things. You have to be able to control yourself; you can't let your emotions get in the way of your mind."

— Widely quoted

ON ADVICE FOR SOMEONE ENTERING THE INVESTMENT FIELD

BUFFETT: "If he were coming in with small sums of capital, I'd tell him to do exactly what I did forty-odd years ago, which is to learn about every company in the United States that has publicly traded securities, and that bank of knowledge will do him or her terrific good over time."

SMITH: "But there's twenty-seven thousand public companies."

BUFFETT: "Well, start with the A's."

—Adam Smith's Money World, October 21, 1993

ON RISK

"Risk is not knowing what you're doing."

—*Omaha World-Herald*, October 28, 1993

ON INTUITION

"In the end, I always believe my eyes rather than anything else."

—*Omaha World-Herald,* October 28, 1993

ON NOT WORRYING ABOUT WHAT THE STOCK MARKET DOES

"As far as I am concerned, the stock market doesn't exist. It is there only as a reference to see if anybody is offering to do anything foolish."

—Peter Lynch, *One Up on Wall Street*

ON THE IMPORTANCE OF ECONOMIC
CYCLES TO INVESTORS

"If Fed Chairman Alan Greenspan were
to whisper to me what his monetary
policy was going to be over the next two
years, it wouldn't change one thing I do."

—*U.S. News & World Report,* June 20, 1994

ON TAKING YOUR TIME

"An investor should act as though he had a lifetime decision card with just twenty punches on it. With every investment decision his card is punched, and he has one fewer available for the rest of his life."

—*Forbes,* May 25, 1992

On the Journey Being the Reward

"In a sense Berkshire Hathaway is a canvas, and I get to paint anything I want on that canvas. It's the process of painting that I really enjoy, not selling the painting."

—Widely quoted

ON PROFIT VERSUS GROWTH

"I'd rather have a ten-million-dollar business making 15 percent than a hundred-million-dollar business making 5 percent. I have other places I can put the money."

—Roger Lowenstein, *Buffett: The Making of an American Capitalist*

ON STICKING WITH WHAT YOU KNOW

"Invest within your circle of competence. It's not how big the circle is that counts, it's how well you define the parameters."

—*Fortune,* November 29, 1993

ON WATCHING THE PENNIES

"The really good manager does not wake up in the morning and say, 'This is the day I'm going to cut costs,' anymore than he wakes up and decides to practice breathing."

—*Fortune,* April 11, 1988

ON WHY TEENAGERS SHOULD START SAVINGS ACCOUNTS

"There's nothing like the savings you accumulate before you start raising a family and the bills start coming in. . . . Plus, the money will work for you for a longer period of time."

—Associated Press, November 11, 1997

ON MOTIVATION

SPEAKING ABOUT ONE OF HIS MANAGERS, JACK BYRNE

"Byrne is like the chicken farmer who rolls an ostrich egg into the henhouse and says, 'Ladies, this is what the competition is doing.'"

—*Forbes*, February 2, 1981

ON OPPORTUNITIES

"Great investment opportunities come around when excellent companies are surrounded by unusual circumstances that cause the stock to be misappraised."

—*Fortune*, December 19, 1988

ON THE VALUE OF PRACTICAL EXPERIENCE

"Can you really explain to a fish what it's like to walk on land? One day on land is worth a thousand years of talking about it, and one day running a business has exactly the same kind of value."

—*Fortune*, April 11, 1988

ON GETTING EXTRAORDINARY RESULTS

"What we do is not beyond anybody else's competence. It is just not necessary to do extraordinary things to get extraordinary results."

—*Los Angeles Times Magazine*, April 7, 1991

ON BUSINESS SCHOOLS

"It has been helpful to me to have tens of thousands [of students] turned out of business schools taught that it didn't do any good to think."

—*Fortune,* April 11, 1988

On Long-Term Thinking

"Our favorite holding period is forever."

—Financial Review, March 17, 1989
(reprinted from *The New York Times*)

On Focus

"We don't believe in the Noah's Ark principle of investing, winding up with two of everything. Then you have a zoo."

—*Financial Review,* March 17, 1989
(reprinted from *The New York Times*)

ON PUTTING ALL YOUR EGGS IN ONE BASKET

"We don't get into things we don't understand. We buy very few things but we buy very big positions."

—*Financial Review,* March 17, 1989
(reprinted from *The New York Times*)

ON THE FUTURE

"I see myself running Berkshire as long as I live, and working on séances afterward."

—Adam Smith, *Super Money*

On Self-Image

"I have always felt I was going to be rich
because it's not that difficult."

—*Financial Review*, December 9, 1985

ON MASTERY

"When I get an investment proposal, I can look at it in five minutes or less. I can filter out 99 percent of the ideas in five minutes."

—*Financial Review*, December 9, 1985

ON LOVING YOUR WORK

"I love what I do. I'm involved in a kind of intellectually interesting game that isn't too tough to win. . . . I don't try to jump over seven-foot bars; I look around for one-foot bars that I can step over. I work with sensational people, and I do what I want in life. Why shouldn't I? If I'm not in a position to do what I want, who the hell is?"

— *The New York Times Magazine,* April 2, 1990

ON WHY HE HAS ALWAYS WORKED

"It's not that I want money. It's the fun of making money and watching it grow."

— *Time*, August 21, 1995

ON THE EXPERIENCE OF AGE

"My God, good managers are so scarce
I can't afford the luxury of letting them
go just because they've added a year
to their age."

—*Fortune,* April 11, 1988

ON PASSIVE INVESTING

"We don't go into companies with the thought of effecting a lot of change. That doesn't work any better in investments than it does in marriages."

—*Fortune,* April 11, 1988

ON THINKING SIMPLY

"There's something about smart people
explaining ideas to an orangutan that
makes their decision-making better."

—*Fortune,* October 26, 1987

ON STOCKBROKERS

"There's no reason in the world you should expect some broker to be able to tell you whether you can make money on index futures or options or some stock in two months. If he knew how to do that, he wouldn't be talking to investors. He'd have retired long ago."

—*Money,* Fall 1987

ON LEAVING EXECUTIVES ALONE

"I found in running businesses that the best results come from letting high-grade people work unencumbered."

—*Fortune*, September 11, 1989

ON BEING A GOOD FATHER

"Love is the greatest advantage a
parent can give."

—*Fortune,* September 29, 1986

ON LIMITING WHAT YOU BUY

"Billy Rose used to say that if you have a harem of a hundred girls, you never get to know any of them very well. The trick is to know a lot about what you own, and you don't own that many things."

—*Financial World*, June 13, 1984

ON BEING CONSERVATIVE

"You leave yourself an enormous margin of safety. You build a bridge that 30,000-pound trucks can go across and then you drive 10,000-pound trucks across it. That is the way I like to go across bridges."

—*Financial World,* June 13, 1984

ON HIS FINAL GOAL

"What I want people to say when they pass my casket is, Boy, was he old!"

—Source Unknown

HOW HE DOES IT

What exactly is up this investment magician's sleeve? What are the techniques
Buffett uses to record stellar gains year
after year after year?

Well, let me be frank up front. It's impos-
sible to give a full course on Warren's tricks
of the trade in the short space allocated here
(for a really sound schooling I suggest you
read four brilliant books: *The Midas Touch* by
John Train[1], *The Warren Buffett Way* by
Robert G. Hagstrom, Jr.,[2] *Of Permanent
Value* by Andrew Kilpatrick[3], and the big
daddy of them all, *Buffett: The Making of an
American Capitalist* by Roger Lowenstein.[4]

[1] Harper & Row, 1987
[2] John Wiley & Sons, 1994
[3] AKPE, 1994
[4] Random House, 1995

What I can do, however, is give you a useful basic guide to the strategies Buffett uses to pave his street with gold.

THINK LONG TERM

Don't get caught up in the frantic whirl-wind of stock trades that captivate so many who play the markets. Rather, take your time, a long, long time, before you invest in a company. Investigate every nook and cranny of its operation. If it has retail stores, go down and check 'em out first-hand. Get your hands dirty. Study every document you can find about your target. Really do your homework.

Forget about the daily fluctuations of the economy and the stock exchange and see the stock market as Buffett does—one overly emotional person called Mr. Market, who gets depressed when things are hard and far too euphoric when things are good. Leave Mr. Market to his own life and paddle your own canoe. Ask yourself, "Is this business likely to be healthy, not just in the next month, or even the next year, but in the next decade and beyond?"

That type of long-term thinking scares the daylights out of most investors—and that's why there aren't many Warren Buffetts in this world.

BUY BUSINESSES YOU UNDERSTAND

Remember his Circle of Competence theory. Step outside it, and the vultures will begin to gather. Stick to investing in industries you know something about. When you have a feel for how the game is played, you're much more likely to score a home run. Forget a hot industry if it's not in your area, even if it seems like a sure thing. Buffett's game is all about minimizing risk, and you haven't a hope in hell of doing that if you've got to learn about an entire industry and every itty bitty aspect of a company; it's just too much to ask.

Part of understanding a company is understanding its management team. Are the executives competent?

Are they experienced? Or, as Buffett would say, are they fanatics? Buffett's style is to keep his hands off the day-to-day running of the companies he invests in, and that is only possible when the people running the ship are committed experts.

When you've done all the hard time and really feel you understand the company you're investigating, it's time to look at what a sane price for it is. Here the key point is margin of safety. Even if every other aspect of a company comes up roses, if the price is not sufficiently low for you to have a real margin of safety in case things go wrong, walk away.

DON'T OVERDIVERSIFY

You can't be a Bo Jackson in investing. Spread your energies and your capital too many ways, and you are courting disaster. If you have really taken your time and only picked stocks that are bona-fide doozies, there's no need to diversify for safety. If you're not supremely confident about the future of each stock in your small portfolio, perhaps you should never have invested in them.

Remember, the fewer stocks you have, the more time you can spend becoming an expert in them. Buffett rarely owns more than ten, and much of his capital is tied to just two or three. Now that's focus.

Learn Basic Accounting

There's no need to get an MBA in bean counting, but a basic understanding of company accountancy procedures and balance sheet reading is a must. There's a lot of smoke and mirrors in the investment world, and many an annual report is designed to deceive, not clarify. Be on your toes for these shenanigans, at least by being able to comprehend the game they're playing.

While it's true that your stockbroker should be able to offer some sensible advice, remember he or she probably has neither the time nor the inclination to dig deep. There simply is no substitute for your own spadework.

COMPOUND!

One of the keys to Buffett's success, often ignored by his appraisers, is compounding. Berkshire Hathaway has given only one dividend; it was twenty-nine years ago and, by Buffett's own admission is, unlikely to happen again. He'd rather reinvest the money and use the miracle of compound interest to his advantage.

Just how powerful is compound interest? I'll put it this way: If you put $2,000 a year into an IRA at age nineteen for just eight years, until you are twenty-seven, when you retire at sixty-five the $16,000 will have ballooned to over a million dollars! You do not need unusually high returns to make good money with compound interest, but you do need to be consistent.

To give you an idea of just how obsessed

with compounding Buffett actually is, let me tell a little story. According to one of Buffett's golfing buddies, Bob Billig, Warren was flabbergasted when he found out his wife, Susie, had spent $15,000 on interior renovations. "Do you know how much that is if you compound it over twenty years?" he spluttered.

That's big-picture thinking. That's Warren Buffett, the greatest investor of all time.